Follow That Star

Matthew 2:1–11
(The Visit of the Wise Men)

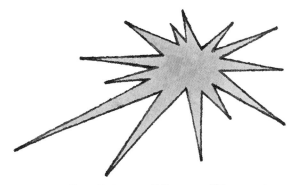

by Mary Manz Simon
Illustrated by Dennis Jones

CPH™

SAINT LOUIS

Books by Mary Manz Simon

Hear Me Read Level 1

What Next? CPH
Drip Drop, CPH
Jibber Jabber, CPH
Hide the Baby, CPH
Toot! Toot! CPH
Bing! CPH
Whoops! CPH
Send a Baby, CPH
A Silent Night, CPH
Follow That Star, CPH
Row the Boat, CPH
Rumble, Rumble, CPH
Who Will Help? CPH
Sit Down, CPH
Come to Jesus, CPH
Too Tall, Too Small, CPH
Hurry, Hurry! CPH
Where Is Jesus? CPH

Hear Me Read Level 2

The No-Go King, CPH
Hurray for the Lord's Army! CPH
The Hide-and-Seek Prince, CPH
Daniel and the Tattletales, CPH
The First Christmas, CPH
Through the Roof, CPH
A Walk on the Waves, CPH
Thank You, Jesus, CPH

God's Children Pray, CPH
My First Diary, CPH
52 Ways to Raise Happy, Loving Kic
   Thomas Nelson Publishing

Little Visits on the Go, CPH
Little Visits for Toddlers, CPH
Little Visits with Jesus, CPH
Little Visits Every Day, CPH

Copyright © 1990 Concordia Publishing House
3558 S. Jefferson Avenue, St. Louis, MO 63118-3968
Manufactured in the United States of America

Library of Congress Cataloging in Publication Data.
Simon, Mary Manz, 1948–
       Follow that star: Matthew 2:1-11, the visit of the wise men/by Mary Manz Simon.
       p. cm.—(Hear me read Bible stories)
Summary: Retells for beginning readers the Bible story about the three wise men who follow the star to the baby Jesus.
       ISBN 0-570-04177-5
       1. Magi—Juvenile literature. 2. Bible stories, English—N.T. Matthew.
[1. Magi. 2. Jesus Christ—Nativity. 3. Bible stories—N.T.] I. Title. II.
Series: Simon, Mary Manz, 1948– Hear me read Bible stories.
BT315.2.S555 1990
232.92'3—dc20   89-35133
                                                              CIP
                                                               AC

4 5 6 7 8 9 10   00 99 98 97 96 95

Name _____

Date _____

Presented by _____

_____

To the Adult:

Early readers need two kinds of reading: they need to be read to, and they need to do their own reading. The Hear Me Read Bible Stories series helps you to encourage your child with both kinds.

For example, your child might read this book as you sit together. Listen attentively. Assist gently, if needed. Encourage, be patient, and be positive about your child's efforts.

Then perhaps you'd like to share this Bible story in an easy-to-understand translation or paraphrase.

Using both types of reading gives your child a chance to develop new skills and pride in reading. You share and support your child's excitement.

As a mother and a teacher, I anticipate the joy your child will feel in saying, "Hear me read Bible stories!"

Mary Manz Simon

For Matthew Michael Simon
John 10:14

Look.

See that star?

See that star sparkle?

That star is for Jesus.

Let's follow that star.

Let's see Jesus.

Bumpety bump.

Bumpety bump they rode.

Where is Jesus?

See that star?

See that star sparkle?

Follow that star.

Bumpety bump.

Bumpety bump they rode.

That star is for Jesus.

Let's follow that star.

Bumpety bump.

Bumpety bump they rode.

They rode to see Jesus.

That star!

That star!

Where is Jesus?

They see Jesus.

Look at Jesus!

About the Author

Mary Manz Simon holds a doctoral degree in education with a specialty in early childhood education. She has taught at levels from preschool through postgraduate. Dr. Simon has also authored *God's Children Pray,* the best-selling *Little Visits with Jesus, Little Visits for Toddlers, Little Visits Every Day, Little Visits on the Go, My First Diary,* and the Hear Me Read Level 1 Bible stories series. She and her husband, the Reverend Henry A. Simon, are the parents of three children.